IF I HAD NOT SEEN THEIR SLEEPING FACES

Copyright 2023 © Christina Tudor-Sideri

ISBN: 978-1-916541-01-6

First edition.

All rights reserved.

First published in 2023 by Erratum Press
Sheffield, UK
www.erratumpress.com

Cover image, design and typesetting by Ansgar Allen

IF I HAD NOT SEEN THEIR SLEEPING FACES

fragments on death after Anna de Noailles

Christina Tudor–Sideri

ERRATUM PRESS

I have seen the inert faces of the dead, in dreams, in memories, in hours long forgotten. In condensed nights and woeful Novembers, in the pleasure of living worlds apart while bound together, in the gentle love of a house in ruin, in attics and all over the body—the body, an *ars moriendi* no paper could endure. One by one or thronged together, the dead come, they come and pretend, for the sake of the living, not to have known love, not to have known life, not to have felt the rush of warm blood through their now silent veins. Today, when death is no longer a part of life, today, when what survives is literature and discourse and theory—today, when death is distant, intangible, when no vocabulary remembers it. I have seen the dead, and on their faces, I have seen the world. The primaeval world, before *memento mori*, before the nihilism that grips us, the world, before the aseptic, before the loneliness of time and its fatal embrace. The whole of the world, on the faces of our dead: a sweet lie one utters to oneself on the verge of sleep, a hand that rocks the cradle; a lie, a modality of expression—stiff, unyielding—if one were to say that expressions require patterns and ways of manifestation, but yes, nevertheless, a lie, this lie: the faces of the departed hold truths beyond anyone's reach, beyond coherence and chronology—no, beyond the consistency of living; truths unknown to those condemned to hold the torch, to incinerate the night in their passing, to search everlastingly for what the dead already found, for what the dead know, and what they carry written on their flesh, on their faces, amidst the lines and folds and wrinkles of their decomposing bodies: that in absence of movement, in absence of warmth, in new colours invading the tissue like small passions flooding the senses, in colours of lips never again to be touched, through the veins of the dead, the cruelty of time no longer comes to meet the waves of the brain. And this, forgotten everlastingly: death.

Death itself, its disappearance from collective consciousness. In its place, a riddle, a lesson, a secret, a sacred plan to be unravelled, a truth to be discovered, yes, that is how the meaning of death comes, a regrettable, insipid, *carpe diem*. What was once known now lies forgotten in the catacombs of a world in so much pain that rushing from one forgetting to the other is the sole purpose of its existence. What was once known—death, for the living, life, for the dead, two oceans never to be explored in full, never to be entered with bare limbs and aching organs. Yet on these oceans, we've sailed, we sail, still, in search of realities, of certainties, in search of lives that escape the mind as soon as they are perceived as being real. Lines and folds and wrinkles and paths cut by time, by nature, by the will to live; markings on the face of the dead, of our dead, our dearest, departed, forgotten—lies and lines to utter and stroke and hold in memory, for what is the world if not the memory of how the dead are forgotten?

No warmth in their weary limbs, no tremor disturbing their slumber. The dead, their dream, an anatomy of paradise and hell and what we know as the in-between, an anatomy, a map of everything we have burdened them with. They sleep, for they have walked and inhaled and exhaled an existence and beyond, in realms just like ours, lands that we now worship—that is how we evoke our dead, as immortal, as coming from a place of wonder, as the inhabitants of dreams, of memories, of hours long forgotten. In the language of love, in the tyranny of chains and settlements, in the indecencies of masks, through neglect, through deliverance, through the sadness of the soul: in the language of death. The dead sleep when the living get lost in the darkness of the forest, they sleep when the living swim their days away, they sleep when the living linger at their gravesites, they sleep when the living come together and say: they have left us, our dead, they have abandoned us to this pursuit, to this necessary search for an end—for the end. All on our own, we walk, we struggle, we redefine rituals and chase away representations of the past, that is what the living say, they speak of taking pleasure in illusions and chasms and houses whose shadows loiter like distances on the barren heart. The dead have left the living, to walk the earth as if nothing recognisable can ever exist, to walk the earth, to go farther and farther from the resting place of silence, to where no flowers can grow from the flesh of those they have loved.

Countless bodies, aligning their bones with the roots of ancient trees, piercing the wooden homes built for them by the living, not with despair, but with the confidence, the faith, of what was once known as love, the faith of an itinerary of unbound desires, in death, enmeshing with flowers above. *I want you to watch over me tonight. I might die in my sleep.* And it is thus that the language of the living washes over the memory of the dead, language and its ephemeral murmur, its blessed offering. It is thus that darkness falls over the ruins of time.

Silence piles up between the air and the waves, silence, as I drown for the first time, for the last time, for all of time, my blouse undone, gasping evermore. Gasping for hands, for words, for skin, unsullied, not by the promise of heaven, not by the cold embrace of the tomb, skin, as I once knew it, skin, as it once embraced me, skin, the discipline of the unruly body. Silence comes and borrows the language of the familiar. It comes and fills the soul, the beautiful soul, the forgotten soul, the invented soul, the soul of nature, the soul of the human, the soul of everything created to withstand the brush of time. Silence comes, and in drowning, I lay a refusal at the feet of death. Never again shall death be studied, never again shall it hold over us the staff of coincidence and happenstance, never again shall there be confusion. No confusion, no piercing nothingness, no departure of sound, no impetuous desire, no terror, terror that plunges one within the depths of one's very heart, where the soul grows so that the body can feel—where I grew, with you, I grew each day, like a book someone wrote: word after word, line after line, page after page; a book that, when finished, was tossed into the fire that was started with the sole purpose of growing, too, of rising and becoming absence, the absence of a book, the absence of a heart, the absence of pleasure, undone, like a paragraph on the skin, the absence of flesh on the bone. Whatever the reason, whatever the ways of this silence, whatever the purpose of why we worship it, of why we speak without words, of vividness, of escaping, of ethereal places not yet imagined, the remedy in this journey, this path, this dance, this touch I dare not compare, the remedy is to walk this path, and, having reached the end, to say: it is not death that I fear, but what I have undone to find it.

I have seen their white faces, their numb hands, I've touched their names, in silvery lettering on crosses made of wood, made to last—made to last as an image in the mind of the living, an image that nevertheless crumbles under the weight of what it carries. As a child, perhaps six years old, perhaps my first funeral, that of a young couple, buried together, hauled at the same time from the fortunes of a life unknown to them, a life that flows and passes now, in death, through bodies void of dream, of future, of any and all fragments of imagination. Consider how a child sees it—death, distant yet a touch away, how a child plucks flowers from the earth to place on two bodies, buried together as the tradition demands it, in nuptial clothing, in fabric embroidered with silk like forgiveness stitched on the heart, their union, their beauty, their disdain, even, disdain for so much imitation and farce and all that lies in the mind of the living when preparing the dead for their final journey, for their forever resting place, disdain for everything that lies in memories and letters and for the voices of those who, years later, perhaps will remember them, and will try to utter it as I have—a funeral, perhaps my first. Come, then, recall the first sight of death. A couple. Buried together. The weight of their absent life crushing them into eternity.

I did not know that one could endure the unacceptable, I was never told, never shown, how gestures travel from me to you, how, sometimes, I can only withstand silence in cemeteries, gazing through an imaginary peephole at accidents from other worlds, my mind rising above, far above the trees and the colours of the skies and the gusts of the wind, above everything there is and above the nothing yet to come—so high up that I can reach them, the dead below, so high up that I can plunge into the depth of the unacceptable, so high up that I can travel back in time, a journey not like everything I have imagined, a journey, not through years, but through touches, and gestures, and ruffled sheets, a journey that goes beneath the transparency of the skin of fruits, that goes to where the demise of the world is but a promise, but a vain image, philosophical decorum, a journey that takes me to a time long before ever knowing how nature heals all that it kills. How nature breathes, and the punishment becomes a gift, how nature touches, and the cruelty takes on the shape of a hand, a warm hand upon the wound, how nature sighs, and intimacy becomes the very act of living, and dying, and being born again, inside a frame that can't contain you, and yet it tries, nevertheless.

How everything ends in this hideous rest, and how brittle the skin—yes, the skin, the skin that prevents blood from gushing downstream when one swims in the river, that keeps organs from rolling downhill when one sleeps amid the wilderness of a summer night. How frail the skin that touches, how frail the skin that is touched. The skin, this skin, which lives for the dance of the body, which lives to remember, and rock itself to sleep. How frail all that ends in such a rest, in this sleep that erases all dreams, this sleep that lures one with the promise of a faraway life, where no rest shall ever be disturbed, and that is what we long for, is it not? a rest like no other, a rest where soporific hands decompose on the tongues of the silent. The hands of time, rotting away on the bodies of the benumbed, on their thighs and around their ankles, on their stomachs and over their eyes. The hands of time, a veil no sight can resist.

I extend, with eyes bent over the abyss, a hand that forgives and one that strikes, I extend my two hands, to death, to dying, to life, to living, to touch and touching, to the watcher in the attic, to the marginalia of the text, to the river of pain that crosses our corroding houses. I caress the arteries that course through the body of the world and I strike the face that dares, the face that thinks to utter words in vain, the face that dares to speak before me with the mouth of all humans who have ever lived and all humans who are yet to be born—the universal voice, the voice that comes and says: your homes are just places where you go to die. This voice, the mystical vein, the ambivalence of how life lasts, and why, of how there are shells born with the sole purpose of being emptied and shells that live eternally, always full, always brimming, through the certainties and disputes of the human, to the end of life itself. And when that end will come, we'll dissolve into each other, this voice and I, this world and I.

So do the days pass, swift and aimless, we call them sweet when they are dreary, we dress them up and exhibit them, we take the hand of a day, and then another—I hold the hands of all days, all at once, my limbs, eternal and countless for this sole purpose, to hold the hands of days so tight that not a single one can escape, so that the skin of all days, of these passing days, turns violet with each new hour, deeper, darker, a shade so violent, a grip so tight that not even the sky could free them, these days that have passed just to end up trapped in the tight grasp of becoming the past of someone human, someone weak, someone passing, just like them, these days, keepers of death's secrets, these days, swift and aimless, these days, that I cherish and I bruise, these days that I hold together like a bouquet of immortelles, as if life itself had stopped so that it could live eternally inside the hollow of my hands.

How short time is, how few brisk mornings, and oh! how little books have taught us. There is nothing gathered inside the mind, nothing on becoming as dissolution, nothing on the reconstruction of a shadow. The book is a mask, a mask concerned exclusively with feeding from its reader. One after another, they latch on, and through what these books promise to teach, through illusory lessons and time that passes and pages that rustle and exhaust themselves—no, that mimic the process of extinction, for the page is eternal—they feed from the mouth they cover, from the brain they fill, they feed on the reader until, on her deathbed, what remains is not the surfeit of having read, but merely the exhaustion of having been consumed.

I carry the fatigue of this ancient messenger, I carry within this needless will to live, this vertigo, on trails and steps, when going up and when descending, this vertigo that I never feared, this vertigo that lives inside of me, which I now speak of like an invocation, as if to awake it from its slumber, this need for dizziness that fills and satisfies me like the memory of a lover. And I, having seen, having lived, having known, having forgotten, I speak as if language itself were sufficient, as if all there is and all that will ever be is the word and the word alone can hold me, the word alone can quench my thirst, the word alone can heal the wounds that hurt but that somehow, I never felt open. The word alone: death. And in it, the collapse of having lived.

Bring the pleading universe under my rule, let it flow, and in this flow, let it gather that which needs gathering, let it heal the world of the temptation of the dying, the allegories we've took for acts of living, let it gather that which can be given to someone who, as ruler, lives herself to gather and utter and rush beyond what can be gathered and uttered and rushed toward. Beyond the gentle fatigue of hours like these, beyond the voices of death, of conjugated paradoxes, in recollections, inside the head, outside the body, everywhere, at once, death, which needs not to respond to our calling. Someone who, as ruler, lives to force remembrance upon the flesh of those who drown for pleasure in Lethean waters. Hedonism, but at its eeriest: to seek pleasure in awakening those who are lost in their own concept of gratification, to seek pleasure in pulling their bodies and uprooting their minds from the soil of what comforts them. To lift them up and away from the warm and the delicious; to do so as to bring them—no, to ground them, in times of horror and mistrust. That is how we rule, those of us who think we have indeed been endowed with the power of caring for others, with the strength of guiding them away from where we ourselves once bled, with the nerve of thinking that our pain is their pain, and thus we know—yes, we know and we can heal, we can provide them with a healing hand, a hand, like a detour to death, a safe passage to where, even if suffering were to reach them, there would be ample awareness as to endure it. That is how we rule, with insolence and naïveté, over the universe that pleads and pleads, the universe that begs for a new path, the universe that asks for new ways of being, while our own world, menial and insignificant, drips and drips and drips evermore from our veins, unknowingly, when embraced by whatever it is that has deceived us into thinking that our theories on time and life and death and how one speaks when one must speak are in fact not theories at all, but reality itself.

I stand before you like blood on the ground, before the cradle and the grave, arms abundant, flowers everywhere. Flowers for the beginning of the world, for hearts that beat and hearts that no longer know how. I stand before you, bare skin and familiar, and on the page, I write that I have never known you.

An endless Babel, scattered across the world we have not yet been brave enough to invent. The image of someone once loved—a human, unclothed, exuding warmth, exposed as if in a shop window, as if on the wall of a museum that never welcomed any visitors. A corpse and a coffin that we do not call *corpse* and *coffin*, for the corpse is the body of a lover and the coffin is the only home that will have him. That is how one wanders the earth, pointlessly, how one projects upon its landscapes the image of life and death, how one teaches the roots and the flowers and, why not, the clouds and the wind and the birds that got swept in such an embrace, how one teaches them of death and dying, the created language of death and how difficult it is to hold it inside the mind, how difficult it is, in the end, to speak of those who perished, to speak in words like *perished*, to make up words and phrases meant to preserve the little that can be preserved, in death, from life. That is how we become moments of being. How the body remains a body.

Thus have the days fled, without my eyes counting them, without my pages being able to contain them. I speak and I tell of memories, memories of dirt and flowers and theories, so many theories, nihilistic visions on the faith of the human, *nihilistic*, because the word fits, the word resembles something familiar; ideas, concepts of how one holds dear and owes—yes, owes the dead, for in their succumbing, they took not the world, but its ugliness. In their departing, they cleansed our souls of what was evil and wicked—and such is said by ancient messengers and voices of the old and wise, and through these voices, tradition carries on, and with it—no, because of it, at its feet, I remain ever so wary to pluck flowers from cemeteries, and eager, oh! so eager, to keep, on my body and in my thoughts, to place at the centre of whatever labyrinth I have formed and twisted for myself, the absence and presence of you, the dead—the dead of the world, my dead, the dead to come. I keep you on my skin, in lines and folds and wrinkles, in words that time will nonetheless smooth back to their primordial shapes, to the primordial shapes of everything that was. On this skin, I keep your touch and the shadow of your breath. In your honour, a living tribute to your memory and the memory of absent hands, I wear the colours of the forbidden. No black, no mauve, not a single shade or fabric that is recognisable in mourning, but colours, pure colours, and thus, the journey becomes my own, and the crossroads—the crossroads, I carry within. To protect this thought, the thought of you, I search in books for words and phrases that speak as if they themselves were tiny humans, that speak and say: *only the dead have lost one another.* I bow and nod my head and I remember that I, too, I myself am washed ashore in the land of the living, I am spit out by the netherworld and exiled from the dead so I can keep alive the thread of blood that pulsates as eternal connection between what was and what is to come, for if I live, so does every thought of you; if I move, so does the shadow of your body.

But I see only abyss, I see terror, and silence, as one sees, perhaps, from time to time, the outline of a return, so clear yet in the distance, gazing back only when the eyes look away. I stand on the bridge between night and day, between dark and the light that conquers it, alone, with thorns growing into my flesh, unable to discern between what I see and what I was told I will be seeing. The air blends with death, and silence falls only to amplify the noise. I am asked to surrender. I am asked to submit to this external reality, to this threatening existence, which nonetheless will injure me. You have not understood the meaning of life, I am told. This is why I flee. This is why we flee from ourselves. This is why we go where there is abyss, and terror, and silence. We are being asked to surrender, to understand, to choose one meaning and abandon all others.

In the blueish hour where man is born, in this very moment, and in this specific time, this epidermal time, time like a syndrome, time like a chapter, in this hour, here is where I undress and gently place the clothes under my head. Here is where I lie, in other worlds, in other manuscripts, and this is how I flow, through other words, like blood through other bodies, how I sleep, alone—how I sleep and speak and say that I have died and thus I can no longer travel toward a sun that would have set aflame my living body.

My heart is like a corpse that has been laid in its grave, washed of sin and delivered to its eternal rest. The first organ one thinks of—the heart. The first smile, the first sway of a swing, the first touch, the first scream, the first orgasm that traverses the body and plunges physicality into ethereal pleasure, into excess, into the eternally superfluous, into love, and potentiality, and the promise of doing whatever the body asks for, whatever the heart asks for, when it lies, like a corpse, in its grave. Give me music, I say, without knowing what music is, without remembering a harmonious sound, give me music, any kind of music, and let us dance to the sound of our denied existence. It has gotten dark. It is dark, and we call it chaos. We call it chaos, for we've been told by someone, somewhere, perhaps when we were reading, or walking the paths of a new city, or tracing with our fingers the maps of others, perhaps when we were taught something—someone, somewhere, called upon our memory of the dark and named it chaos. This wayward darkness. To tread this semantic territory instead of dancing, instead of swaying quietly, left to right—indeed: chaos. How deep can one go without thinking of a world devoid of humans? Beyond voyeurism—how deep? How deep can one imagine the unimaginable? The sea recedes and the image of the world cuts to a body on the shore. A film memory: birds against the open sky. A world without humans. A world seen by humans. A metamorphosis, everlasting, for there is no end to something one has created in the mind, and neither death nor life can rinse the shoreline of this distance. The distance between the end of the world, imagined, and the I that imagines it. A distance that perhaps could be the most faithful depiction of closeness one can ever put on paper. Beached, abandoned, the body imagines a world without itself. Within it, the heart imagines a world without the body.

Holy oils have penetrated my bones, and I, much like yourself, know now that I have given my life to illusory paths. Artificial and erroneous, misguiding and misdirecting, paths that I've followed at night, only at night, obsessively repeating the names of holy oils to myself: the oil of the sick, the oil of the catechumens, the holy chrism oil. Impossible to know now for what purpose, to know how it comes, and why, and when to say: enough. Impossible to end this unfortunate affair, to condemn this endless grief, impossible to confide in you and speak of what I foresaw, speak of what was to come, to say that this is not a poem, that this is not an essay, that this is not anything, but a mere heartache on the page, a river flowing nowhere, humbled, frightened, knowing nothing of what originated its misfortune. I am counting on you to know, to understand that all such delays are like tight embraces that rob one of all air, embraces that hug and hurt the body with a passion no healing of pain justifies. Impossible to know for what purpose. Paths that I have lingered on excessively and always in vain, paths I have abandoned so that today, in this hour and in this space, to be able to write of them, to be able to say that I, much like yourself, have given my life to the unreal.

I breathe and you are sleeping—at night, a canvas painted by a filmmaker, someone who holds the brush as if holding a camera, who records its strokes without knowing what language they speak, what life they live once they are there, on the canvas, on film; a filmmaker, if a filmmaker were to have painted, if her hand were to have reached beyond the comfort of ink and the ardour of film, if so, perhaps, this would have been an image, a landscape, a twisted portrait of two unrecognisable bodies, apart, one above and one below, an image born from the stroke of a writer, a filmmaker, a painter, a night admirer, a carrier of rain. This image: I, breathing; you, sleeping. Apart, brought together against nature by the gentle hands of someone who could have perhaps painted us in such a manner—but we do not know, and so we return to our sleep, each in our own world, we return to our places of rest: I, in my bed, you, in your beautiful wooden box, and we utter, there, the one to the other: how beautiful you were. Far from here, you are sleeping, in foreign lands that have been kind enough to welcome your confused remains, in cemeteries— yes, cemeteries, for that is how I always remember what I have not known of you, that is how I imagine what is left of you, testimony to those final wishes, I imagine pieces of yourself in all corners of the world, for you have always wanted to know, to write, to decipher, beyond the maps of my skin, what happens to the scattered soul, what happens when, or if, by chance, the body were to loyally follow; if, perhaps, the body too were to scatter its limbs far away from one another, as the mind does, at times, with its thoughts and memories and ideas on the meaning of death. The body, with its arms apart, one above and one below, like two beings who loved each other too soon and not for very long.

And I know that for the dead no other time exists, that there is no respite and there are no philosophies to frame the measure of such absence. I know that for the dead no life exists. For them, for the dead of this world that frantically carries on outside my window, for the dead of my village, for the dead of the streets, for the dead of my childhood, for the mediaeval and the modern, for the dead as form and the dead as desire of return; for your dead, for them, I have carried waters through snow and hail, through stifling suns and parching stretches of summer that went on and on as I grew and grew. I have carried the waters of the dead without ever dipping my fingers to moist my thirsty lips, I've carried them beyond the shadows of their haunted houses, beyond the graveyard cross—for there is but one cross and all other are mere projections—I've carried them as tribute to the human, to the elsewhereness of primaeval times. Let me come, let me again carry the waters of the dead and let me pray, now that prayer is nothing but a halo to put on and take off like a crucial experience of life, to pray not as I have been taught, but as I please, not how I prayed when such teachings were all I knew, when the narrowness of the world and the vastness of death allowed for nothing else but reaching out for the hand of He who made me, but how I pray now, when reaching for the body I can only touch in times of prayer.

The dead remain dead, and the living are tired from having seen so many times on their cold faces the fate that awaits and overwhelms them, the living, yes—the living, who, in their infinite detours, know not of death; the living who come together and share stories of angels descending into the abyss to pull each and every lost being, all lost souls, from its depth and darkness, one day, when the time will come, and angels will miraculously manifest out of thin air and walk the earth as it has been given to us. When the time will come and the living will have forgotten—they will have forgotten that time, as time does, cannot just come, that time has to leave, it has to pass, and it can only do so through trees and bodies and through whatever else lingers in its path, be it the image of an angel or the absence of a death. They will come, the living say, the living who come together and speak of how the time will come, time that will stay, time that will burn those worthy of burning, but not them, for no time can touch them—time that will stay, for the world does not know, but time too is weary, time too is tired from having seen, on the faces of the living, the markings its lashes leave in its passing.

The hopeless void where souls are not, the firepit, as it has been described to me, the residence of hell, but not hell, a barren land, from where every evil has been banished. Earth. In photographs and films and literature, drawing out one's sensations and fears, preparing the human to witness extinction. Startlingly bizarre, erotic, comforting, always dominant, this vision of how the world must end, the texture of the skin, a mere memory in the crevasses of the wax figures we leave as testimony. This array of lines and references, marginalia, falling, turning, transfixing, stretching from film to hand, from wind to mouth—together, a monument of openness toward an erroneous outcome, a caress of an untrue contour. When swimming in the sea, when reclining, when lakeside and serene, when writing of the fall into oneself, of death, when saying, as others before have said: I am dying, and this *I*—this *I* that has died will never die again. When held, when absent, when emerging from the womb. There is a void and toward this void we march, eager for erasure, nervous and uneasy, ever so keen on confronting the unknown that once cradled us.

Your delirium is mine; I know that we begin anew, I know that what was said no longer is, that what was dreamt has vanished like a portrait of the self, a damaged depiction erased by the passing of time. I depend on the narrative of others, but I know, and reveal myself in this knowledge, not through thought, but through storytelling. I resist the making and the unmaking, and, with great patience, I tell stories— stories that suit me, stories that remember you, stories that are more beautiful with each inconsistency. I know, and in this knowing, I afford myself the favours of corrupting not one heart, not two, but all of them. I continue to live and write and tell and take advantage of how dreams come to me, how you come to me, like the sea, like the city, like the years of euphoria you've dreamt but never lived, like the capital of the soul in the middle of a labyrinth undrawn, unexpected, a labyrinth so small that no one but myself can imagine it, like the hour and the minute and the possibility of another touch, another quarrel, another existence—the whole of another existence, haunted or serene, precarious, or sharpened by the knives of the eternal. However way it comes to me, this knowledge, however I think of death, of the instance when God existed and played for me this song, this opera, when God existed solely to give me this glimpse into a new beginning, however such recollections unravel, in excess or scarcity, in drunkenness or consciousness, in a multitude of obstacles and trappings and flowers on the grave, I know that your delirium is mine, and through it, we begin anew.

I carry the weight of time and the heat of summer like wreaths on my head, I carry them, and I think: I will soon be drained of all will. A *tableau vivant*, a remodelling of shapes that have been in dialogue with one another for too long, like water lilies enthusiastic to the touch. How does willpower come into being if not by way of illusion? One could even venture as far as to call it tradition—yes, the tradition of pursuit, of being seen or unseen, of choosing the realm where to survive or to vanish, the bodily languor with which to walk the earth, the conscious return, even the words one must speak. The tradition of will dominates the scene, a reverie, if ever we knew how a reverie comes to us. What a reverie is, for us, those who often drown in its existence. Looking back and looking onward, a flesh figure made of brushstrokes, intimately gazing at time, at seasons, at how they all paint the world in colour and nostalgia. A woman embracing her lover. A standing body, a reclining nude—a thought, revisited, remodelled, reshaped, redirected.

And I breathe with a weary heart, I breathe, and I stretch out my arm through forests and into the waves. And there is no greater landscape. No other more beautiful than this scenery made of words: I know not of myself. I breathe, and I unfold like a canvas put away, like an untold story of flowers and belonging to the earth. I settle only in dreams and instantly allow myself to be absorbed by the labyrinths of sleep, by the trails of silk and hair and arms stretched between death and the ripeness of all seasons. No greater landscape, no other experience, no other more beautiful than this: the street I walk, the embrace I do not escape from, the forests I pass through. A moment of dormancy that comes to me as an image of beauty, like a white, lathered sea, like desire, and expansion, and excision. *Devour me*. In dreams, I say: devour me. Dressed in the darkness of the night, in the tendency toward decay, when no exposure truly matters, I hear myself speak as if I were another, I see the coloured buds tucked gently between my fingers, as if floating above the body. The body in sleep, the body in death, the body in decomposition.

Earth, take the dead, be gentle with their dreams, carry them to where lashes still flutter, like in childhood fairy tales, take them to where mouths still enjoy the bounties of your soil. Take the dead, with their cascading black hair, their shoes like marble tied to the feet, their mannequin-like figures, their minds, their fingers, in bed linens, in baths, in subway stations, in museum darkrooms. Take the dead, arms around the waist, corpses on the medical examiner's table.

Like a child embracing a devious beast, I pause and gather my words and phrases together, ceremoniously, as if I were to place them inside a picture frame, as if I were to make of them a photograph, to make of them, to make with them, a symbol of pulsating life and wetness and hell, an image of noise and undoing and suffering, tumescent, quivering, an image of water swirling upon the eternal stone.

Night brings the living and the dead closer together, and it is at night that we allow the dark to fall over our eyes in flesh, and fabric, and waves. Docked like a boat in the water, the body feels at home. The stroke of the wind, this ever-present surrogate for a caress, for an embrace, for a word that could perhaps explain why there is a body, and why this body feels at home in the tomb, why this body knows not, admits not, that the tomb too shall be empty one day. The wind that comes and takes from my arms this death that I have been carrying for so long, it takes it from me and hides it into the attics of the world, a world no longer eager, no longer willing to pretend that death exists. A world living outside of its own contours, outside of its own light, which, at funerals—at its own funeral, flickers gently in the hands of a stranger, for only strangers can hold and carry the light of the dead. My faith is a candle no one remembers to light, my faith in why and how I heal—my faith, when alone, when the scream, the inner scream collapses inside of me and creates a void, a vacuum so consuming that the whole of the outside is dragged there. Something deep and dark and unrecognisable. Something no manuscript should concern itself with, for no book is able to bear the weight of what it cannot say. My faith, a mere belief in immortality, for what is more ordinary than to think oneself eternal? A black veil over the face of this abyss—dirges and lanterns and rites of passage as the soul becomes a bird and the bird takes to the sky. Such faith, the faith in the garden flower that will grow again. At night, my faith puts on the mask of your face, as I once knew it, immortal and endearing. Such are the faces of the living wearing the masks of their dead, the faces no death anthropologist would dare gaze at on the cross. I take a black pen and circle on my skin: spots, discolorations, scars, the memory of hands, ties, reminiscences of rope, the flowers we hid between the seams of our clothes and the lines of our bodies. Darkness falls, and from a notebook, the faded scribbles of our first death remind me of my faith, which no one remembered to light.

From our rising houses to your sleeping tombs, the vertical and the horizontal, the living and the dead, the trembling metaphor of why we live, and how, and for how long, of how we strive for a good death, the kaleidoscopic haze of what remains on the path once we shed our febrile skin in a miasmic atmosphere where everyone has been asleep for ages and the only sound a heart makes is that of the pen touching the page. There would be no history, there would be no past, there would be no death, if, from time to time, we would not shed our skin on whatever path we happen to find ourselves travelling.

May their gazes remain alit on my face, may I remember the dead, I say, may I remember them as I remember the living, languorous and volcanic, sensuous and nostalgic, slipping between images in the mind, filled with life in their bodies, brimming with thought and handwritten text. There is an unspoken rule to life, perhaps a means, a map toward the quickfire of understanding, a rule that says we must obey the fallen and the falling, a rule that says tenderness is dependent on linearity and to linearity it owes its shards and fragments being held together. A rule that says one does not remember whether time passes in a straight line, a rule one mustn't follow, a rule that says all is lost when the mind encircles itself.

Chopin! And we mourn the happiness that was denied to us—music, and we prepare for rearrangement, we take photographs of how we were and then we place ourselves at the mercy of this river that will remake us, this projection of life rushing through the veins, life that in its passing rearranges the cells in the body, life that returns, time and time again, only to cast us into someone new, as if it were a child, unsatisfied with her creation, a child with the whole of time at her disposal. And then, the child becomes a memory—the memory of a child and the memory of time and that of rearrangement, when swimming, when reclining, when serene, when music floods our insides, in beds and on sofas and lakeside benches, ongoing and utterly hypnotic.

You remind me of music, of sounds, of chatter that the night has placed before me when, with eyes closed, I took a photograph of my damaged body and held it up to the sun, waiting for it to reveal not the present, but the silk ribbons and red hair of my first years, the red mouth and open eyes—eyes contemplating the world and themselves, almost as if they were able to see beyond what the mirror and the photograph show. I took a photograph and searched in it for geometric shapes, for memories of buildings that follow the contours of the body like an embrace, for wooden boxes that call upon the flesh. What does one see in a photograph of oneself? The heart, buried deep inside the body, alive, lively, like ink on the page, in outlines unimagined, the heart, reminiscent of erotic dimensions and rooms where music and books, and the very best of what we know so intimately all linger in the air, existential and incensed like an imaginary muse passing through, whose hand you wish to hold but whose ghost makes the body tremble. An image of living and sleeping and dying; an image of feeding and bathing and moving through a room where music abounds, where the clamour of voices is but a distant memory. In the night air, on the path where no traces remain, rendering, uttering to yourself that which is most urgent: the word is everlasting.

Yet you shall be dissolved, my glowing heart, you shall become grass and water, and in this becoming rests the hope of the world, this becoming, a washing of the body in the river; the body, sometimes a tapestry, other times the box that encloses it, removed from all the geographical aspects of its past. The body, the life and death of the body, eternal motifs, repetitions, on each page the same thought, the same burden, the same pleasure. A line runs through the night; lines, fading wrinkles on the skin of darkness; a line, drawn, expected, erased, foretelling the return of gestures, since gestures and gestures alone can heal one when the heart dissolves and the body becomes a wave in the night. A hand gesture—supine yet immemorial. The body, once flesh, the hand, once writing, the mouth, once calling for embodiment to be displayed in the window-shops of the world. The once lived, now eternal.

Midnight strikes from the dark clock of a convent, and I, alone, having renounced the world for the thousandth time, concern myself now with impressionability. I urge myself to become malleable, to lie in bed and let the waters of the mind carry me away. All is love when the letter is pressed upon the skin. All is precious when the caress mimics the fleetingness of time. All is in vain when one thinks of death.

Hiding my ardour from the gaze of stars, I look at the page, I look at my skin, I contemplate what lies on the ground close to my feet and all around, lovers asleep, letters unopened, contact between film and skin, differences—the abyss that separates us. At night, exposure takes on the role of an emotion, and even though it matters not, this exposure, it comes to us like a final basking in holy water of the body that is no longer a body. The repeated body, the overcomplicated body. That is what I see, my gaze averted, in memories, in premonitions, in dreams of other days, I see time that went by and time to come. The repetition. I see clean clothes, limbs tangled, bound together, I see your coffin facing east. The pagan and the religious, embracing each other in this image, this funereal appearance that lives inside me like the word. This appearance that unravels now in letters and sentences to echo fragmented voices from afar.

What am I to do with you, who are ephemeral? With memories kept in boxes, with stories I've burnt only to read them again and again. What remains of the vigil, the here and now of the gathered emotions and materials of passing death, for death too passes—these candles that we've lit someplace else, sometime in the past of another life, these candles that I have been carrying from room to room, like tiny ghosts between the fingers, these candles, from year to year, from life to life. *May God forgive her.* Endlessly—this forgiving. A death grant, of sort. A good tradition, what one utters, what one does. A container, placed in the room where the coffin is laid to rest; in this container, the living put their hopes for the afterlife, as if throwing pennies in a wishing well. It bores a hole in the table, this container, this vessel that no word can properly name, its heaviness reaching inside the very core of the earth—an open wound through which faith itself falls, and falls, and falls, until it finds something lenient, and drinks it up. Until it fills itself with forgiveness. This container, a boat that takes to the sea and drinks up and is content.

With time that swings but does not flow, time, like a scarf around the throat, like a message that says: remember to live, memory takes its rightful place and thus ceremonies flood the land. Alms—and we are close to the dead. Closer, perhaps. I am like all women; my reflection outlines the night in unseen shades of sea and wildflowers. *She has died on the shore.* An epitaph like a portrayal of annihilation, quickened by the sand and the waves, incensed by the wind and the burning sun. A fragment of death, repeating itself *ad infinitum*. Resplendent life rests here, in the creases of my skin, in the hours of my clock. Time is the painter, and I, its model. I enter in dialogue with the eye behind the camera, with the mind behind the page, with the hand behind the canvas, hoping to be afforded this one thought: I would like to reimagine and restage myself. Now, in these final hours, now, when approaching anything other than sleep makes me more vulnerable than ever. Undercurrents, streams, stories that gush forth from the mind, untruths, pale like the breasts of the model, still, adamant, same as the landscape they helped create. I accept to pose further. Time asks, and I say yes. Instead of well wishing: *May God forgive her.*

Why this abundant murmur of fountains? I see it, I do not hear it, I see it like in a black-and-white film, it looks at the camera as if it were human. As if it were searching to capture my gaze. I see it, and I am engulfed by an inexplicable need to be loved. All from this—water, fountains, the echo of rivers and seas. An elegy for the ways in which I live. Against the ways in which I live. Flesh and bone, life and death, myth and reality, body and corpse, recurrent dreams—no, themes, voiceovers: closeness. Floating in mid-air, this murmur, this sound, alone in the universe, alone in the film, alone inside the chambers of the heart, this hum that circles the world, this pathos, this morbid reflection on the state of memory and daybeds, this rapture that caresses the skin and weaves the hair. A language, a silent language that you nonetheless see, not hear, when you are lying on the bed, when you are on the ground, gathering the seeds of flowers, when you utter the word *home*, and a strand of hair strokes the face. An image that speaks of the origin of the world: water, susurrant.

Bring waves and their foam to my feet, I long to travel—I long to travel and then to come and tell you that I have seen the world. I long to find your grave, and there, next to your name, eroded by the wind, by the rain, carved by the falling tears of those who knew where you were resting, to let silence embrace me, to let silence fill the gap of these years, fill the void, the error—so easily forgotten—the error of farewells uttered before the time of farewells had come. There, to make from grief a map and show you how I've travelled, how I disappeared and reappeared, to tell you that the earth is beautiful, and cruelty is nothing but a fading memory. There, at night, to tell you that I will leave again, that no voice will ever again utter before me: do you repent? That there is no sea that will not welcome me, and no grave left unvisited in search for the ruin of you.

To these young warriors, who won the battle by succumbing, in this chronology neither of us recognise; to them, to us, I speak of unconsciousness and chiaroscuro and the blood that comes from poems and stories invented by bodies and the silk that caressed them. Poems that capture the flush of the cheek, the pulse of the hand, the warmth of the skin, the thorn of the rose. And isn't that why the human speaks, why the mind thinks, and struggles, to make sense of death? To know where the body goes, to know how the heart throbs when life is no longer. To know why death remains a concept. Torpor—when reclining, when resting, when dying. And in it: a sky of flesh. Not the end, but the beginning of silence.

What did you want? What mountain, what peaks? What tomb attracted you? What death wish did you harbour? And how am I to question this, how am I to question that which one pretends to know, how to return and hold in my arms that which I have so ferociously abandoned? No return is ever possible, for no past remains unchanged, no corpse preserved, no gaze alit. And that is how conversation happens, when we speak to ourselves, when we understand not the dark, but its absence, when we touch not the one who sleeps in our bed, but the last refuge of this effort—the effort of touching, of loving, of asking the dead about their death wish, of retracing a life now ended, this effort of writing everything, for only through writing one can exist to the point of wanting to know, only through writing one can pause, and remember, and savour moments, virtues, desires, lost bodies. Only through writing, can one climb the peaks of existence and break the silence of death. Only through writing can the faultless receive their penance. Only through writing one can create paradoxes, little paradoxes, repetitions, only through writing, one can say it all, one can say the same thing, only through writing can the idea become a language, and the language a skin.

Be absent, if you will, be a stranger, lost in sleep; be present there, in the lines with which I describe distance on maps and photographs, be the arm outstretched toward the untouched body. Be what you will, but let me lie here, with my face hidden, let me make use of whatever hours are left in order to erase the discomfort of sleeplessness. Let me lie here without speaking of great loves and hands of mechanical bodies that never learnt how to touch. Let me lie here, next to your absence, where the body is still, where there is no peril in such a stillness, no death in the absence of movement. Beyond these details, further, let me imagine warmth. Beyond death, let me imagine the dead. Let me say that absence has become a passage through nonexistence, and in this passage, the earth, above and below, has been severed past repair.

Here is the shepherd whose dream is haunted, the sole remnant of ancient times. We know of him from the tales of the village, we know of him not as a human being, but a character invented when someone, anyone, tried to preserve the image of the days in which we ourselves were created. We know of him and his pastures, we know vividly, the colours, the sounds, the gait and the pauses, we, the children, know—knew—movement, and thought, and how there, at the edge of the forest, he wanted to rest, but the tale did not allow it. We know of him, the shepherd, we know his dreams, we know his death. The good death, that in the end, matters not to those who have named it such, for there is no understanding, and there is no lesson, in myths, in tales, other than this one lesson, if lesson must be called: there are others—there are others, and through them, alongside them, life is lived and lost and mourned as it always was: not as lesson, but as remembrance of humanity.

And here am I. I hold no wish and I carry no grudge, for I too am invented. I, too, come from other times, like a ribbon around the neck—a repertoire of other thoughts, other bodies, other wishes, of rocks pushed together by the sea. I go on speaking. I speak for the first time. I speak no more. I say nothing of white sheets, of night like a scalpel, of marmoreal hands and splayed legs. I leave it all to the manuscripts about death, that is what they speak of—what they make of this eroticism, of this image, the image of atemporality and how it too perishes in the anatomical. When the model dies, the picture takes its place, yet what we see in it is not death, what we see is love, and that is what we learn to speak of: no longer death as discipline, no longer death as theory, but love—love, the condition of nonbeing. That is how we learn to speak of our dead, when we capture them in photographs, we speak of love, and our words create a living abyss, an abyss we must thus adore, an abyss we must gaze at and admire, a source of pleasure—the focus of thought itself. That is how we invent death, how we forget and call it love, how we look at the dead and see them not in coffins, but how they once were, in beds and on sofas, on the beach and in the gaze.

Disillusioned bodies consent to death, it is said; they abandon their limbs to decay. Perhaps, yet they do so by offering us an authentic trail to follow, a documentation of life as they lived it, the abandonment marks the way, their fatigue becomes our guiding light. There is an unspoken rule when writing about death: nonlinearity is the rope that holds us from falling. Another rule, in disagreement with the other, now forgotten; another rule, foretelling those to come. We live to make sense of rules. To trace life, chronologically, to trace life as such is to offer from the very beginning the idea of death on a silver platter, it is to say: I know how this ends, and so do you. There is no metamorphosis, no understanding, no cinematic revolution—all is present, there is but the need to utter it, to write it, to give it shape and form it to the liking of whomever asked for it. Always how it happened, always hiding the truth of what remained unlived, unrevealed. To narrativise death is to betray life.

Poor human hope, at last, you are no longer able to faithfully attempt this intrepid climb, at last, I can say that I pity you and not the other way; at last, I can claim, with no misgiving, that it is you who are bound to perish. I let the thought slip from the mind, with the sole purpose of banishing it; I let the body tremble at the thought of pity, and I think of cities on the water. I think of reflections, of mirrors, of how I've cherished hope, always, enough to let it fall without condemning it. I wish this away, as well, and feel now the embrace of another layer of the past, something undamaged, and for that, forever unremembered.

The tomb devours and eats away at you, the tomb, laced with disregard for the living, that is how one thinks of it, that is how one shapes in the mind this thought of the eternal home, how one allows oneself the idea that the eternity of death is but an illusion, like a driveway in the forest, deformed by one's expectations of it. The moon has turned red, and I am plagued by other thoughts, yet death lingers still, and I say— no, I think: I could never hold the falling body. I have been trying to escape it, this past that once was, but not for me, this past I was oblivious to, ever since I was made aware of it, ever since, as it happens with lives already lived, it unravelled at my feet like fabric rejected by the body. I locked myself in a room and stripped off everything that reminded me of train tracks, of forests, of boulevards and cemeteries, of sun and cities and seasons—of time itself. I stripped of time to empty myself of the distance that made possible for such a veil to fall upon my eyes. For days, reclining, lying, snapping my fingers as if that is all it took, sometimes bruised, sometimes written on, a wax figure bathing herself in the waters of amnesia.

Yet my heart comes every evening to contemplate your ruins, your buried bones, your ashes, your burning vessel on the water. The empty bed, unmade one day, prepared as if for a ritual the next. And I know that it matters, that for this conversation, for this journal, for this fragment, it is important that the return happens time and time again, that the body, unscarred and unadorned, returns to the place where death embraces the mind and makes from it a landscape of oblivion and make-believe. I address you, and I plead forgiveness from the reader, that in order to emerge from this state, to return from the night in which I came to see you, in order to leave the train, to exit the station, I must imagine, time and time again, that I did in fact come, that I am in fact writing letters, fragments, words that meet on the page in order to become a story I've convinced myself needs telling, that I must repeat, incessantly, how I dared to let this loss wash over me, how I have sought, as anyone would, a way out of an unwelcoming labyrinth. I must imagine that such a thing exists, that I care not of death as I encounter it in the histories of others, but of the death you placed like a child into my arms, and in doing so, created this promise, that I will come, time and time again, to contemplate your ruins.

Like a loose link in the chain of time, I take a step and then another, and thus remove myself from the grasp of the wind. A surrogate where its lashes touched: words that breathe gently upon the skin, as if gods were guiding them, teaching them to move in such a way that they are no longer words but mouths that blow warm air over the hidden world of the mind, over measured time, over existence itself. *Death is nothing to us.* The dead lie in their beautiful boxes, there are flowers everywhere, and death is nothing to us. That is how one finds oneself trapped inside the theoretical, inside the discipline, inside the conversation that happens eternally, how one replaces the wind with the thoughts of others, thoughts that teach us about endings and beginnings and how they fade from the mind when we say this: death is nothing to us. This conversation that holds at its core, as if it were a cradle rocking a sleeping child, the ever-present cradle, the metaphor for all things entrapped, the concept of end days. But the end becomes a poem and floods life with recollections: cemeteries, shovels, dirt—dirt thrown on the dead of others, beautiful wooden boxes, flowers, childhood. An endless array of breathed moments and imprinted traditions, superstitions, misconceptions, all returning from a time that yes, perhaps agrees with this: death is nothing to us. I take one step, and then another, and return to a time when I, a mere observer, a face in the crown of mourners, there, on the edge of the freshly-dug grave, was oblivious to the nearness of death. I undertake to put into words the very meaning of this, the purpose of thinking, of agreeing, of confronting it, the sentiment behind these fragments, yet I cannot do so without being confronted myself by the reality that one cannot truly utter, one cannot say with certainty what death is. Beyond the scientific knowledge we hold of it, beyond the toils and torments of how it marks us, when it comes, when it opens the door to our home. Beyond all that, can we truly know what death is? Can we know enough to say: death is nothing to us? In an attempt to rationalise the irrational, we repeat it obsessively: death is nothing to us. We place it at the core of our existence. We hide it in between other fragments, other stories, other lives. At its origin, a means to eradicate fear—the fear of death, now, a language of its own. A language which we call upon as if beckoning a vessel to shore. A gesture. A slight-of-hand trick to carry us until the embrace of darkness is no longer feared. Yet through this language, and in this gesture, we speak not of how we have thus abolished fear, but rather, of how we have transformed ourselves into its myth.

In spite of my outstretched arms, in spite of hands that have turned pale from waiting in the cold, I still pursue this great vision: the gesture and its memory. I weave together line and thought, I read and agree with the words of others: yes, *our grammar of death must be revised*, I give birth to conversations—with the dead, with the self, with the ill body, with the dying form, with the world, as tribute, and, why not, as companion for when time will again find itself in that moment, companion to the self who stood at the edge of the grave and knew not how the coldness of death would come to strike her face. The perspective of this, of the gesture, of how I remember it—the perspective of any and all gestures becomes wide enough so that anyone can find something in it, so that, when mirroring our days, the denial no longer weighs on the body, and the gesture itself can thus travel back to when it felt familiar. The gesture and its memory, a testimony to how one thinks, and why must one adhere to thinking, to knowledge, of the self, of the other, of what is to come, a testimony that there are indeed end days, yet how one will live them is beyond that which constitutes such knowledge.

The day has come, and I said nothing, the day was here, and I hid my face, I altered my voice so as not to be recognised, as not to be another who knew, who always knew: the day will come. The day has come. The amniotic no longer protects.

I gazed at flames and ignored the ashes; I looked fire in the eye as if it were a creature. No, I looked fire in the eye as if it were a person, a human of flesh and embers, standing before me, a vulnerable body, porous, full of longing, an apparition of times passed, a daydream that speaks of the meaning of carnal remembrance and of how eagerly shadows fall upon the flesh when one emerges naked from the waters of this living picture.

Here is your thunder, I say to the world above, my body knocked sideways by its might, the might of a thunder whose echo I can no longer hold in my head. It is another who needs to hold it in my place, but others are in various states of sleep, of death, of nonbeing, they're tangled in different stages of grief and eroticism and life—reclined, so that no thunder can strike them.

Take your dead on the road—a plea, if ever there was one, a plea to carry and care for the dead as we once did when they were leaving, as we did when we knew that death was near, for death does not come unexpectedly, the lore tells, and I remember everything about it, I remember all that humans have created in this act of trying: to convince ourselves that death does not come suddenly. A plea to write the book of dying, to leave to those who come from us, to leave them words on how to die, on how to craft such lives that when death comes, it will be gentle, that when death comes, it will not strike, but rather carry, and caress. Yet what we left, what we wrote of, were traditions, and rituals, and manners for us, the living, to handle the passing, manners for the living to know death, not as it comes, not as it takes the other from our bed, but how to treat it, what to give it, how to urge it—how to make death not come for us. And it is this coming of death that most occupies the pages of what we leave behind. This coming, and what prophecies it. I remember: the household objects, the chairs and tables and cabinets and how they are meant to rattle and whisper, I remember the foretelling shadows on the wall and how glass is meant to break as if by the hand of man. I remember the icon, how it will fall, I remember how doors will open on their own. There are signs, and some of us know how to read them. There are signs, and these signs say: death is coming. Death has arrived. Take your dead on the road.

The time for scattered dreams and silence is upon us, black spots have surfaced all over the skin, and all the waters of the world have taken to their depths. It is thus that time returns, it is thus that it has come to pass: a brief mention inside a journal, a poem that wishes to become a dream, something we write down in order to remember, to think of later—we, the surviving, later, when time can once again be counted by the hands of the clock, when its passing is not a storm, but the memory of one, and we sit by the fire, at night, retelling of how we were brave enough, wise enough, shrewd enough as to survive it. Black spots surface all over the skin of the world, they are our manuscripts, the books that speak of how we lived to know a time beyond the time of the dead.

And I no longer listen to your Elysian voices, I no longer dream of paradise like I did in childhood, when it was promised to me, this garden of heavenly delight, this realm where no sinner shall enter. I closed my eyes one day, and I imagined it. I imagined its waters, its flowers brimming with colours and sweetness, I imagined all there was and all that it could be, and there, in that beyond, on the edge of the untold, next to what was never pictured, amidst what was never explained, I saw it, I saw paradise: I saw darkness driven away, and light blinding us all.

The night floats, softened, austere, taciturn, imperious, she is funereal, like an urn, she places herself in my arms with the haste of a being eager to be a part of life, night and her shadows and veils and hands that fall upon the eyes so that the mind can imagine, so that the mind can dream and see a world unlike any others; another world, each night, with each dream, a new city, a new sea, the smell of river water on the skin, the sight of forests everywhere, or nowhere at all. It can be that, nowhere, it can be nothing at all, the night offers it to us, to those unwilling, to those unable, to those in need of silence, and emptiness, and dreamless hours. Night comes, it devastates us, and in its arms, the body rests.

I think of the dead, for whom it is neither early nor late, who have no more wishes, no departures and no shores, I think of the dead and the sea in which I swim becomes the earth in which they sleep. To carry such a necessary deficiency within, to belong to thought and thought alone, inside oneself, this bitter deprivation of taste and touch and mad youth, to cost one tears and days and life, for life itself is lost when no departures and no shores remain, life is lost for the living same as for the dead, when it is neither early nor late, and imagination is the sole carrier of one's world. The mind rehearses, it measures and acts out and creates for itself a life before the real that is lived, experienced—the mind travels through time, in an instant, and finds there all that is, all that can be, all that will never happen as so many things do not happen, not in life, nor in death, but the mind knows, and it gives them to you, nonetheless, your actions, your choices, it places at your feet all that could be, and thus you swim in this sea that has no shores, no islands, this sea that offers nothing but the illusion of the lighthouse of reason, which you swim toward as if climbing the crest of a mountain, a thousand times a day, you swim to escape the suffocating hold of this insufficiency.

It seems that we have now seen the worst, I write, night after night, the same thought, and this journal becomes a reality, it becomes written in a time when, yes, we have indeed seen the worst, and so, having seen it, we understand; we say to ourselves that it has become as clear as day, we, the humans, we, the survivors—such a great task to accomplish, to find, to see, to understand, to return to beauty what beauty has given us, and to do so in the midst of terror, in the midst of pain, confident that what our hands gather is what was once given to us, neither willing nor wanting to see it any other way. We have seen the worst, I write, when death comes, when I take a turn and the path becomes another, when the day lingers as shadow on the face of the night, when tenderness, and passion, and long absences trail each other under your footsteps, one by one, little by little—just think, these conditions, these illnesses that come to entertain the heart, reminders that the savageries of life are always followed by the peacefulness of death, like works of art from so long ago, engravings, reminders of the transience of life, and how it is most natural to take everything it gives you: all bodies, all travels, all unions, in daylight, at night, never careless, never repentant, to take it all, though thousand more will follow, yet the hunger is eternal.

The living are silent, but the dead have spoken, that is how myths are born, that is how we unspool the ball of thread, how we make sense of difficulties and voices and gazes averted, that is how we grant and how we refuse, how we love and despise, how we are soft, and weak, and pleading, how we remain. That is how we constantly remain in the land that rejected us: we tie ourselves to the dead, for they have given us knowledge that no living beings could gather on their own, the dead have given us the roots of life.

I look at the immense vault where mortals have suspended the vows of their vain hope, and I wonder, what use could one make for such metaphors, why speak as if one is myth and tale and invention? Influenced by tendencies and language that was given to me, guided by the hands of time, by the footsteps of ancestors, by everything laid before me in the hour of my birth, I trail paths like errors of the mind, I reach for independence, and eccentricity, and the unconventional, without realising that these too are but definitions given to me, that these too are words, improper words to use and speak of death, and dying, and of how cemeteries have become these anonymous institutions where the dead go to be forgotten, where we send our dead to punish them for having left, for having abandoned us, or even, for having loved us, for having rocked us to sleep, institutions of decomposition where we send the dead as to no longer be aware that there are no more eyes, and there is no more flesh, for the body is anything but eternal, and loving it only makes its demise come faster.

Our inexhaustible tears gush forth as though pouring from severed veins and arteries, and at this crossroad, for only at a crossroad there is bounteous time for pausing, only at a crossroad can one stop to mourn the dead, only then is wailing permitted, at this crossroad, we see as if in mirrors, thousands of mirrors all around, the face that no mask is able to keep hidden, we see how truth burns a hole through the body—each truth, a new hole, each truth, a minor death.

Whatever grief is upon me now, whatever force is guiding me to rummage through the mind and gather memories as if they were pearls, to gather and hold together recollections of a past so distant, so absent that one can barely perceive it, whatever virtue or vice pushes the soul to seek these lands, I say to it: come, see me now, look at these words I hold like flowers, take them all, one by one, and make with them a story beyond all stories, make from them a wreath for the head of the body that the sea was kind enough to keep afloat.

In these horrid days, in summer, in winter, in any season, in all the seasons one no longer remembers, there is tenderness and there are torments, there is nourishment, and excess, and perhaps a bond, unbreakable, a bond like a conversation, like a thread, a river, a line of water running through the world, gathering in its path the afternoons and the follies and the pleasure of having sought moments like these, gathering the lies the world tells itself, that God permits these elements to ravish and enrapture and overcome the human and the animal and everything else God himself has created, for it is God who knows, and God who wills it, what is to come, and how we are to receive it, as His faithful children; it is God, the reason for illness, and it is God, the writer of death.

I return to you, ardent and monastic, I return to say that what lies beyond the gates of the mind is something you might never encounter, I come, and I say—no, I plead with you to bear in mind that time is never willing, nor able, to show us everything. That there is, everywhere, and in all things, in life, in light, in literature, in day and in night, under the skin and inside the mouth, in the root of trees and the wings of birds, everywhere, there is an object, physical, imagined, created, a metaphor, a reality, a tradition, since the familiarity of such words might be a good companion to the mind, there is, in all things, everywhere, a return one desires and a return one will never accomplish, and between the two, a gesture toward the self, a gesture toward a being that encompasses the whole of time, that crafts becoming, that cradles nonbeing, a gesture that can comfort and wound and do all that a creature longs for, when, while in the world, someone comes before them, and says: time is never willing to show you everything.

Since I could not prevent these disasters, I lie down as if outside the body, I wrap myself in silk, and I remember that I once cared enough for silk to write and say: in silk, the body falls for its captor. An obsession with decay that invites the thought that nothing matters for the one who knows how to nourish such distressing passions, that for the one who obsesses, the object of their obsession is of little importance; there will always be a will, a way, and a disaster, regardless of the symbol that births it, regardless of vanity, or death, of whether there are serpents, temptations, or poisons, of whether there once was heaven, of whether the body knows— the physical, material body—how to quiet the mind, when it obsesses, when it swims in the waters of rivers guiding it to the beyond—such a beautiful imagery we've crafted, like a still-life painting that nevertheless moves, that nevertheless holds movement, the movement toward death, not of the body, but of that which carries it.

And then suddenly, the storm was over—the storm passed before I could gather my thoughts, before I could travel this path from beginning to end. Before I could admit, to myself, and to the world, that indeed, I cherish endings and I long for their arrival, I search for them in books, and I invent theories regarding their creation. The storm passed before I could write down that a collision is always needed, collisions guarantee an end, and the self—this current self—hungers for the end of the journey. This self that knows nothing of how people lived in other centuries, nothing of how they carried themselves, their souls and their bodies, nothing of how they dressed their wounds, this self that knows not of prayer and solemnity, and macabre dances, this self longs for the end to come, so she can chronicle it, so she can outlive it, so she too can become someone who, beyond the assimilation of death, of illness, of blood flowing through the body not to enliven it, but to gather from it all that is definitive, and abrupt, and without precedent, can sit by the fire, at night, and speak of the end that came and succumbed under the stroke of her fingers.

May the words she uttered be understood by her alone, may these words never be written, never taught, may no translation be possible, and may no remembrance draw them from where they lie in hiding. *May no medicine heal, and no kiss warm the body that death has taken from the world.* A curse, perhaps. An unwritten will of the evil, and wicked, and petty, a manifestation, an infection, like most manifestations, a plague upon the skin of the world, this memory, that there once were curses, uttered at midnight, above fountains, in forests, in the church backyard, under the watchful eyes of the priest who knew that the village needs what God cannot give it, and so he too dabbled in black magic, magic of any kind, for when there is pain in the world, when there is pain centred around the home, one ventilates the rooms not to invite merciful deities, but to make space for those who know how to wound, how to punish, how to give back what was taken. To live in such a world, to know death in such a world, becomes ever more complicated when the one who lives is a child, and the child longs to absorb all that happens around her, the child longs to repeat, and mimic, so that one day, she can be herself. It is thus that death can come to be known, even when it is still a stranger, through curses, and spells at midnight, in the forest, when, again, an observer, perhaps in hiding, the child hears and sees the world for what it is.

Earth, I have loved your blue canopies, your gentle hills, your comforting waves, and if I come to you now, if I come and tell you of your wonders, it is not to seek guidance, but to remember that I was once afraid of water. Nothing but this, a memory so simple, so small, that nothing but its presence can fill the mind, nothing but its strength can heal the body. I was once afraid of water.

On my hand lies your cold hand, so that I may live, so that I may feel, one day, the absence of your flesh, so that I can reach for another—for another hand and another distance, and another loss, another image of the dance, the mediaeval dance of death where hands barely touch, yet nevertheless, they reach one for the other; two, four, countless, eternities gesturing amidst a world that does not know how to interpret—no, that does not know how to allow their presence.

By the complicity of time, that is how all is permitted, how all comes to be known, how one speaks, and learns, and tells the world, through the gentleness of time, time that comforts us, time that deceives us, time that borrows the gusts of the wind so it can speak and tell of how it matters not whether we live under the reign of its measure, they matter not, the clocks we've made, the void they make when they don't strike, the soundless hour, minute, second, when death stops the clocks of the world, when breathing stops and one no longer hears the hour. Yet time, as motif, does nothing of the sort—as motif, as trope, as literature, and theory, and idea, time does not address us, it does not open such possibilities before us, rather, in studying it, time becomes death, and death becomes, again, inaccessible, intangible, it becomes this far away presence, whose markings we feel, on the soul and on the body, yet there is no proper menace to its permanence, for we don't think of it as eternal. We do not think of time as ever-present, but rather passing, we do not think of death as always by our side, we do not see cemeteries as homes the way in which we see our houses and apartments and whatever dwellings we occupy for however long. In studying it, whether time or death or any other presence outside of the proper grasp of our hands, we make from it a notion, a concept so accurate, so meticulous, in the countless theories we develop around it, in the ample ways of observing and speaking of it, in all the questions and through all the answers, even in the absence of answers—even in this, the universal *we*, the *we* that one despises, yet language offers no alternative, or rather, the mind allows for no other alternative but this comforting *we*, for we are many, and all of us swim in the same waters—through all this, time, and death, and whatever we now call *philosophy*, the philosophy of how we live, and why, and what else is there, here, or anywhere, we remove ourselves as presences, as acts of life.

Ruthless Eros presses on my eyes, and hands descend over desire itself, over the longing for death, and in their falling, I ask myself how is it that we wish for death, how is it that the mind performs this trick; I ask, even though I know, or rather, even though I've come to feel it, I've come to experience understanding through what indeed the mind places inside the head, thus, inside the body. I know, yet still, I ask, when seeking pleasure, when feeling, when longing, whenever something small and gentle and almost invisible brushes against my skin and unnerves a storm within—I ask, why death, why this longing for nonbeing, for stillness. If I were to open myself to the perspective of this craving, if I were to write down all manners in which it can be analysed, perhaps I would not linger for too long on antiseptic aspects, but delve deeper into how we understand eternity, time, and that which ends, but also, perhaps the most important of these interrogations, how and why we are drawn by the unknown, not as surge of possible knowledge, not as nourishment for life, but the unknown in which all life ends. How, when thinking of death, in the embrace of lust, under the influence of a thought or a wave or a hand, too present as for the body not to be moved by it, what comes is this desire to know it, not from manuscripts, not from dreams, not from how fear places it at our feet, but rather, to know it as she, death, will one day know us: vulnerable, exposed, full and hollow at the same time. To encounter death in the same manner as death encounters the dying human. To stand before it, not with the purpose of striking her face, not to murder it, not even to question it, but to look at it, to see her frail body, her skin nearing transparency, to reach for her trembling hand, to touch her forehead and brush her hair, and in that very moment, with a mere gesture of the hand, to free the mind of everything, to push away this image, and see it, see this desire for what it is: a mirror that reflects back all that is human, a mirror that places before one's eyes—eyes veiled by passion, and desire, or perhaps by pain, and loss, and utter torment— the realisation—no, this recognition: all that we create, we create in the shape of the human.

May death hide your face, perhaps an old saying, perhaps something misremembered, in this poem, and in the mind of the child, perhaps something to balance the curse, as the world is both evil and kind—may death take from you the face that you are ashamed of, may death wash over you and clean your body to the bone. Imagine that I have lived like this, as well, with the charms and the pleas, with God, with death, with whatever forces and powers and creatures roaming above the heads of humans, that I have lived with the holy oil cross on my forehead, the prayer in my hand, with flowers around my waist, with scraped knees and skin red from the sun. Imagine, also, an outpouring of weakness, of vanity, of possessing and needing to be possessed, a misgiving, an error to think like this, to seek the cure and crush the dream, to split the world into good and evil, curse and charm, life and death. To make of living a binary routineness, to make of resting an opposition of torment, to make of separation a veil over the dying face of love, to have each and every thing, every object, every being, the paraphernalia of breathing and dreaming and touching and swimming in the sea, to make of everything, to make for everything, an opposition. To create dualism, utter intransigent, inflexible, dualism and call it progress, for now you have something, something you yourself have created— your mind, your body, your hands, have made these two things, and then two more, and so on, and through them, the world can understand that it can be both beautiful and foul, both good and evil, both living and dead, but never at the same time, never a variation, never the in-between, never the not created, the not imagined, never the new, never the ethereal. Imagine it as such, the sadness of it being so—that all there is must be discovered, that everything created must be opposed by another, that all questions must carry inside them their answers. That what is human is the body, and what is human is the soul, and there are ways and paths and theories for how one survives and the other doesn't, there are concepts and essential wordings and ideas for how one decays and the other grows, but never the willingness to say: what is human is meaningful enough.

Alas! All is love or ash, all is love and all is ash, nothing remains outside of it, the fire left nothing but this rather innocuous observation, this thought that deludes and bothers us, an idea, forsaken, like an unhappy passion: all is love; all is ash. A meditation in all directions, addressing all manners of living and speaking and being, through which one could perhaps highlight the vital gaze, a collective gaze in all directions, eyes open at once, the eyes of everyone, staring everywhere, seeing the world in all its sadness, seeing love, and ash, and knowing that in saying *all*, so much remains on the outside that one could gather it, for days and days, and have another *all*, and then another, that this is how life is lived, through the little that piles up, through the everything that comes and comes and sometimes leaves, through things and actions and gestures so small that one barely sees them, but, if gathered— if an attempt at gathering them were to be made, one would see that it would last a lifetime, and it would perhaps be the most beautiful way of living, existence in recognition of the *all* that is, the *all*, so little that it could never be gathered, and counted, and named, and so we call it *love*, or we call it *ash*, nevertheless, we live it, unknowingly, or forever absorbed by the light it shines upon our bodies, at night, in the morning, in the middle of a monotonous afternoon, in beds and on sofas, when lakeside and serene.

And we shall become this forest of corpses, we shall be this solitary space, where roots are constantly spreading yet no one witnesses their growth. In the hallways of the dead, where the living keep watch, where there is mourning, and the smell of candles subjugates the nostrils of children who had come there out of curiosity, out of duty, out of love, we will sprout from the earth there, amidst the crowd of humans, around the coffin of the dead, our roots everywhere, shattering windows and knocking over all objects, our roots, the mark of immortality inside the houses of the dying, slipping down—no, up, gushing toward the blue of the sky, connected, aligned but twisted, a symbol of nonlinearity; our roots, a non-narrative, the body itself, the eternal body of nature, our roots, this vision, this monument that shades the very night which created it, silently, in the mind, in transport, in despair, this vision of us: a forest of corpses.

So go the humans tolerated by time, carrying their shadows and hiding their wounds, living as they were taught, an image of impermanence, of transit, of exile, this image, that time holds us in its sways, that it allows us to travel, to seek safety, to seek comfort, to abandon a home in search of another, that time tolerates, and perhaps, through this endeavour, it learns, it moulds itself to the necessities of the human. A creed that, no matter how peripheral, that is, no matter how peripheral its reality, serves to properly understand how, as humans, as beings who move, who create, who impact the earth in unimaginable ways, we would want to see ourselves as creatures who also leave a mark on time, even on death, since we speak in the present, emboldened by the myriad ways in which the body can now heal, of how death has adapted to the ways of the human. One might even go as far as to say that it is not time, nor death, that tolerates humans, but rather, that humans tolerate time, and death, and everything we call *phenomena*, that it is us who make space among us for everything that is and ever will be. As humans, we fall so easily into this slumber, in which we dream of philosophies of essentiality, ontologies of human existence and how everything that binds us to the world, to other creatures, to nature, to inanimate objects is something we can easily modify, influence, change, even sever, if the need were to arise. How easily we fall into this slumber, this dream that wounds us, this dream that casts an invisible shadow upon the body, a shadow that nature can nevertheless see, like a mark that lets it know we are damaged, a symbol of our majesty, as we think it. The surface of the sea cannot exist without water, but for the human, water itself cannot exist without the gaze that captures it, and thus, these ontological ties, these binds that bring all that there is and ever will be under the rule of the human, for the human can see it, the human can experience it, the human can study it, these ties, weaved together, eternally, fall like nets, entrapping us, one by one, away from one another, entrapping us under an illusion of our own making. The world, bound in space and time to the dying human, to the gaze cast by the decomposing body, all ontologies inbound to the fleeting human. And death? Death as reality, death as it happens to the body, not death as concept and theory and discipline. What becomes of such death? A motivator, a monumental presence that reminds one that all life must be touched and discovered and influenced and, why not, eradicated, if need be, by the human. That is perhaps why souls were born, immortal souls, that is why the few who knew our mark is nothing but the shadow we carry, the symbol that speaks of our ruin, created the soul, everlasting, so that sufficient time may pass, and in this passing, the soul can learn to love and seek and desire, not as ruler, but as a mere breath in the lungs of time.

To fall back into the earth, having dreamt of heaven, to fall and to sleep a sleep so deep that no thought can pierce it. To fall back into a place one has never visited, yet a place whose familiarity was imprinted from the moment of birth, a place mentioned by prayers, the depths of the earth, perhaps a hell, perhaps a mere representation of death and how it robs one from life, regardless, a place to where one falls, so perhaps, yes, a hell, since heaven requires an ascend. Yet both, heaven and hell, the world after death, a realm we are meant to know, a realm we are meant to return to, and in this returning, to be flooded with memories that we carried within but never once experienced in life, when the breath was regular and the body warm. Nothing but poetry can describe it, nothing but poetry can hold tight to this presence, to this manner of speaking, nothing but poetry can take the wretchedness of what scripture after scripture has wished upon the human, salvation or damnation, both equally reprimandable, both revolting in how they parted the good from the bad. Yet the poem—the poem can speak of heaven and hell, for the poet knows that what we make comes from within, and what we make wears the same mask we wear, the poet lives and breathes and warms himself by the light of the only necessary truth, a truth repeated yet never acknowledged: the hand cannot cast anything but itself. Repeated, *ad infinitum*, itself, the repetition, a manner of portraying it.

Who could decipher this silent night? The attempt itself becomes a riddle. Small, silly, even, like the riddles one tells a child, not because she is a child, but because she is growing, and is avid to learn, to know, and small steps are the best steps. The silence of the night, the night that is silent, devoid of sounds and echoes and murmurs, a riddle for the mind of the child, who nevertheless cries, and sighs, and laughs; a splendid laughter, a burst of laughter that fills the night, the night that, thus, cannot be silent—a riddle: what silences the night? How is it that there is silence? In dreams, perhaps, through dreams, the night is silent. But does the dream not sigh? Do dreams not become echoes in the mouth, rushed breaths and sounds made by the movements of the body? The night is silent in death. Not because there is no sound, not because there are no echoes and no murmurs in death— because someone once left it that death is achievement, and ever since, there has not been a way for the mind to hear and grasp and understand such a triumph. No sound of death is registered as such, no inevitability, no termination plays for us the proper sound, an echo that would be accepted, a murmur that could make one say: death is an achievement. And thus, the night is silent. A riddle, as silly as the riddles of the child. In death, we sleep and dream a silent dream, for the body does not move, and the soul knows not how to render the afterlife.

It is a distant reminder of early hours, that which holds us here, gazing aback, in the least possible of states. That one is even able to remember, to contradict oneself and the world, and say: yes, I hold inside my hand and within my grasp the memories of primal times, and through these memories, I invite stillness in the body. Perhaps the only state of the living that could afford it, the only state which could allow the lack of movement for so long that one might find oneself on the verge of death, yet alive, still: when flooded by memories of primal days.

And I know that I, having contemplated these remains, having thought and written these words, having travelled these paths and denied these truths, I know that I too shall die, and in that death, I will exhaust all denials, in that death, no refusal shall ever be repeated. In thinking, in writing, in tiring the hand through these repetitions, through these maps that guide one toward the same death, toward the same end, different yet so similar in their purpose that only one could be read, only one could be travelled, studied—the destination is the same. And yet, the path, the time it takes to get there, all that exhausts you on the way—all this is different, and it is in such difference, from such difference that we take our daily nourishments. There could be no poetry without the repetition of a thought that struggles to understand itself, no poem without the madness of a day that strives to become night, and does so by repeating it to itself, over and over, the invocation, the calling for darkness. The mind, when it thinks, when it speaks of the body, of decay, of arms outstretched, of waters and waves and how the whole of time courses through the veins of the body—the mind, when repeating itself, when creating a world just to forget it and start anew the next day, the very next second, that is when the mind is most alive, that is when the mind becomes a body, when the mind feels, when the mind becomes a skin and this skin experiences something no thought could ever experience without living with the circularity of itself: the warmth of breathing—constant, repeating, regular, breathing. That is when the mind sees that death is not something one never encounters, but rather a mere lack of breathing, which the mind cannot know, until it feels it on the skin.

I am the watchful, the insightful witness of the fervent hour, and to myself, to myself alone I say: no one can be recognised under too bright a light. It could become a play, this struggle for affording oneself another moment, another consequential moment, when observation, and experience, and the lived and the encountered take on the shape of light—light above us, light under our feet, light all around us, light to guide our way through the darkness, light to gift others, light to make us see, light to banish all fears. Yet very little is thought of too much light, almost like a superstition, one cannot speak of an abundance of light, one cannot abuse the gift that was given and call it harmful. I interrupt a thought and stitch it to another, to a memory of reading somewhere that the eye can only experience beauty through light. And I wonder, could it be possible, in writing, at least, that the eyes absorb so much light they become themselves a light source, a lantern, such as ancient philosophy describes it, perhaps, light emanating from the eyes and illuminating all surroundings. That one can be a beacon, and for this purpose, there is never too much light, there is never too much one can absorb, in order to see, in order to offer the gift of seeing. Yet, what is there to be seen under so much light? No—nothing can be recognised in too bright a light. Beyond it, in its absence, in the absence of light, there is an abundance of life that one cannot ignore, there is, in darkness, as much life as there is death in light.

Of souls that do not linger in despair, from souls that always find comfort, from those who believe in the absoluteness of any moment, from them I draw my contours and proportions, from them I take my shape so that I'll know, so that I'll have an unshakable temple in which to reshape myself. From those who live in absence of misery, from their houses, I gather stone upon stone to build this illusion, to build a home that gives me shelter when the moment comes, when I will want and long to abandon the present once again, to create a self that holds all matter, a self like space, a plenum that no emptiness, however small, can ever inhabit. It comes to me that it must be thus: to come from the homes of those who do not linger in despair, from what they touched and what they built, from this I can build a temple to fill with a self, and then another, and another, until no error can mark the mind and no wound can be dealt upon the body.

And just by breathing, I create within myself, and in the world, a compendium of the unsaid, where one can hide and shelter all thought, of birth, of life, of senescence—a guide, not on how to die, not on how to discuss death, but a testimony that it is in our metamorphoses and our differences where one can sometimes find the greatest comfort, and through these differences, we know that how we live and how we die, how we carve our attitudes and chronicle the histories of our dead, remains important not because it is meant to come together, to merge with everything that resembles it and become one indistinguishable whole, but rather, because it is meant to be different, and spread over the world like a blanket, to be real, perhaps less theological, less surgical, less scientific. It is meant to be a journal of how we breathe, when we are born, when we live, when death arrives.

I drink the blue that pours from your face, from your eyes exposed, from your mouth agape. I drink the blue and marvel at how liquid the sky feels, how wet and sweet and appetising the gaze that no longer is. How beautifully we speak of death, how marvellous the artistic discourse, its aesthetics, what wonder—disastrous consequences, all throughout history, all throughout time, chronicled in such beautiful imagery, with meaningful intent, even, if values were to be redefined and attributed based on how one depicts hunger and war and plagues and death, based on how fast cemeteries get occupied, and the quivering swiftness with which flowers wither in vases, when night comes, and no rain washes over them. There is, in this language, in the manner in which we strive to understand that which we will never experience, in this language I have fallen prey to time and time again, a beautiful yet terrifying negation, a paradox, but only if our definition of paradox would be slightly different: if the paradox were to become a touch and the touch an absence and the absence a body in the arms of death. And through this negation, through this beautiful knotting of the tongue, one knows that there will always be poems, that there will always be music—yes, and books, and paintings, and guilt, and torment. There will always be death.

I taste this brazen drunkenness, and from it, I take not what I need, but what I once gave to the world—I take, and I take, and I smile, I smile though no one is meant to smile, in words, in fragments, in manuscripts, in passages to be revisited, I smile how perhaps one is not allowed to smile even in journals, where the intimacy of the page guarantees, if only for a brief moment in time, that any action, any gesture, any feeling, any confession is permitted. I think of resurrection, of a judgement day, of how one speaks of rest—eternal rest, and yet the body, for its sins, is never allowed to rest, the body, for its sins, lives and dies and rests in death under the thread of punishment, of fire—of pain, everlasting.

And I collect the voices of the many, a promise of a return, the return of the dead to the realm of the living. Something folklore knows all too well: one day the graves will open. The spirits of the dead will rise from their wooden homes—no, enough: from their coffins—and join their loved ones in life, in celebration, on the eve of a holiday. Always on the eve of a holiday. All through the land, the language of a fairy tale, the living will welcome the dead with food on the table and love in their hearts. It is how we dream of it, how we celebrate it, how we long for it to come, the day the graves will open, and the dead will come, if invited, if welcomed, if the living left them a sign, a staff thrusted into the soil of their eternity, a staff that spirits will use to roam the streets and find their way back home, a staff that they will use to defend themselves from those who are as evil in death as they were in life. The dead will come, and they will assist the living, it is expected of them to provide this assistance, to heal, to bestow good health, prosperity, to enliven the fields and the cattle and also, to punish enemies, to marry women with good men, the dead, in exchange for alms and prayers for the salvation of their eternal souls, they will come, in the eve of a celebration, and heal the living. And then, for the dead cannot be allowed to live amongst us, they will be forced to return to their graves; the living will dance, they will shout and make loud noises, they will use whips and bells and cries, so that the spirits will rush back in fear, back to their coffins. In winter, the day the graves open, followed by the night when the sky, too, breaks open, the night when one is believed to see God sitting at his table in heaven, the night when, through the burning of treasures—no, when treasures ignite themselves, that night, by the light of their flames, people will no longer need the dead. And from that night on, there will be no need for a god.

Those who have reigned over hope like victors know now, or perhaps they have always known, for how can it be that the dead can teach us what they never knew—they know that it is not the body that preserves life, and it is not the mind, either, they know that life is not to be preserved, that forgetfulness must wash over each and every one of us, and that is how we'll linger, that is where we'll live, when no life is possible, and no death remembers us.

But now comes death, with its awful, calm sea, where ships have neither sails nor shrouds, and the veil falls to my feet as if it were a dark wave coming to greet me. I return to you, no longer able to hold you in my arms, no longer able to utter your name; I return to you and say: how beautiful you are. A figure, detached from the time of your death, no longer contemplating abandonment, a body no longer in pain, for that is what we always forget about death, that there is no more pain, no dissecting, no exhaustion, no separation between one breath and another, for there is no breath, and there is no rhythm, and space is but an imagined dimension, and not something one needs to fill. With the calm of death comes confrontation, the realisation that what was emptied will remain such, that what is lost will remain lost, the intimate, the domestic, the wild, the material, the otherworldly, all will remain as the dying mind last experiences it—for the living, as well, like an exhibition trapped inside a time that does not pass but also does not paralyse, inside a time shaped like a home, an apartment in which one dies, over and over again, and everything that was seen last remains trapped; everything that was felt last, by the living, by the dying, by this extra body that the two create, a third body to occupy the room, a third body to see what the other two are seeing, to feel what the other two are feeling, the body of the living-dead, the body that perhaps can preserve warmth, and convey texture, this third body, an illusory mimesis, vivid, nonetheless, and full, and yearning, and loving, everything that this body sees remains trapped, awaiting oblivion. A third body, between the living and the dead, a body eventually forgotten, for, somehow, it had no hands, and how can one remember that which does not touch? The apartment itself—perhaps an apartment, perhaps a house, perhaps a beach, secluded, cold, a cradle, but malleable, wrapped around reality like the most durable of intimacies. Now that I have returned, now that I see you, now that I have travelled the world and have stained my hands with ink and the dirt of so many cemeteries, I return to you and say: how beautiful you are.

A vague murmur emanates from the silence, its presence potent enough to hide my breathing, for I breathe, still, I breathe with the waves of all seas, of these seas crashing and becoming one at my feet, these seas of different colours, different tastes; I breathe with the waves of these seas, and I breathe through the roots of all trees tugging at my chest. I am at home, and I breathe, no matter for how long.

At last, I mingle with these funereal remains, at last, I can admit to myself that I too will know death, for I have dreamt it time and time again, and I have felt its touch upon my skin, its coldness running through my veins, yet I have never known it, and thus I allow the mind to encounter it, I allow the mind to imagine it, to mourn its absence and write of its arrival. The discipline of death. A symptomatology, a lesion, an illness no therapeutic sea can wash away. I let the mind do what the body cannot. *You are not allowed to die.* A voice comes now from the depths of whatever memory I hold eternal, now, at the end, before another beginning, a voice that utters the same words, words that once occupied a reality too full to hear them, a reality much too full to understand them. Words that were said aloud, or perhaps written, or whispered in the dark, words that come now as memories and caresses and reminders that they were once uttered, words that were erased by death itself. In the now that is eternal, in the now that is here, and in the now that will one day come, these words, your voice, from a time so distant that one must perhaps bottle it, study it, a time no past can bear, and no future remember. *If one wishes to forget the dead, one must look at the moon through a sieve.* This tiny fragment of lunar lore, now, at the end, rushed, for there is a beginning that has been waiting, a beginning, lenient, humane, that lingered for years, waiting for these gates to open and be closed by the very hands that drew them. Your voice: one must look at the moon.

I have seen the inert faces of the dead, 1

No warmth in their weary limbs, 3

Countless bodies, aligning their bones, 4

Silence piles up between the air and the waves, 5

I have seen their white faces, their numb hands, 6

I did not know that one could endure the unacceptable, 7

How everything ends in this hideous rest, 8

I extend, with eyes bent over the abyss, a hand that forgives and one that strikes, 9

So do the days pass, swift and aimless, we call them sweet when they are dreary, 10

How short time is, how few brisk mornings, 11

I carry the fatigue of this ancient messenger, 12

Bring the pleading universe under my rule, 13

I stand before you like blood on the ground, 14

An endless Babel, scattered, 15

Thus have the days fled, without my eyes counting them, 16

But I see only abyss, I see terror, and silence, 18

In the blueish hour where man is born, 19

My heart is like a corpse that has been laid in its grave, 20

Holy oils have penetrated my bones, 21

I breathe and you are sleeping, 22

And I know that for the dead no other time exists, 23

The dead remain dead, and the living are tired from having seen so many times on their cold faces the fate that awaits and overwhelms them, 24

The hopeless void where souls are not, 25

Your delirium is mine; I know that we begin anew, 26

I carry the weight of time and the heat of summer, 27

And I breathe with a weary heart, 28

Earth, take the dead, be gentle with their dreams, 29

Like a child embracing a devious beast, 30

Night brings the living and the dead closer together, 31

From our rising houses to your sleeping tombs, 33

May their gazes remain alit on my face, 34

Chopin! And we mourn the happiness that was denied to us, 35

You remind me of music, 36

Yet you shall be dissolved, my glowing heart, you shall become grass and water, 37

Midnight strikes from the dark clock of a convent, 38

Hiding my ardour from the gaze of stars, 39

What am I to do with you, who are ephemeral?, 40

With time that swings but does not flow, 41

Why this abundant murmur of fountains?, 42

Bring waves and their foam at my feet, 43

To these young warriors, who won the battle by succumbing, 44

What did you want? What mountain, what peaks? What tomb attracted you? What death wish did you harbour?, 45

Be absent, if you will, be a stranger, lost in sleep, 46

Here is the shepherd whose dream is haunted, 47

And here am I. I hold no wish and I carry no grudge, 48

Disillusioned bodies consent to death, 49

Poor human hope, at last, you are no longer able to faithfully attempt this intrepid climb, 50

The tomb devours and eats away at you, 51

Yet my heart comes every evening to contemplate your ruins, 52

Like a loose link in the chain of time, 53

In spite of my outstretched arms, 55

The day has come, and I said nothing, 56

I gazed at flames and ignored the ashes, 57

Here is your thunder, 58

Take your dead on the road, 59

The time for scattered dreams and silence is upon us, 60

And I no longer listen to your Elysian voices, 61

The night floats, softened, austere, taciturn, imperious, she is funereal, like an urn, 62

I think of the dead, for whom it is neither early nor late, who have no more wishes, no departures and no shores, 63

It seems that we have now seen the worst, 64

The living are silent, but the dead have spoken, 65

I look at the immense vault where mortals have suspended the vows of their vain hope, 66

Our inexhaustible tears gush forth as though pouring from severed veins and arteries, 67

Whatever grief is upon me now, 68

In these horrid days, 69

I return to you, ardent and monastic, 70

Since I could not prevent these disasters, 71

And then suddenly the storm was over, 72

May the words she uttered be understood by her alone, 73

Earth, I have loved your blue canopies, 74

On my hand lies your cold hand, 75

By the complicity of time, 76

Ruthless Eros presses on my eyes, 77

May death hide your face, 79

Alas! All is love or ash, 81

And we shall become this forest of corpses, 82

So go the humans tolerated by time, 83

To fall back into the earth, having dreamt of heaven, 85

Who could decipher this silent night?, 86

It is a distant reminder of early hours, 87

And I know that I, having contemplated these remains, 88

I am the watchful, the insightful witness of the fervent hour, 89

Of souls that do not linger in despair, 90

And just by breathing, 91

I drink the blue that pours from your face, 92

I taste this brazen drunkenness, 93

And I collect the voices of the many, 94

Those who have reigned over hope like victors, 95

But now comes death, with its awful, calm sea, where ships have neither sails nor shrouds, 96

A vague murmur emanates from the silence, 98

At last, I mingle with these funereal remains., 99

Christina Tudor-Sideri is a writer and translator. She is the author of the book-length essay *Under the Sign of the Labyrinth*, and the novel *Disembodied*. Her translations include works by Max Blecher, Magda Isanos, Anna de Noailles, Mihail Sebastian, and Ilarie Voronca.

PREVIOUSLY PUBLISHED AT ERRATUM PRESS

The Prodigious Earth
Eric Blix

Morant
Roy Goddard

Last Days of Pompeii. Vol.1
Steve Hanson

bone bite snare
Michael Mc Aloran

PUBLISHED BY ERRATUM REPRINTS

The Scourge of Villanie
John Marston

Civilisation Its Cause and Cure
Edward Carpenter

www.ingramcontent.com/pod-product-compliance
Lightning Source LLC
Chambersburg PA
CBHW030306100526
44590CB00012B/541